Desktop
RUGBY

EVE LEGATO

T0364004

ISBN 978-0-7624-6091-5

Running Press Book Publishers
An imprint of Perseus Books,
a division of PBG Publishing, LLC,
a subsidiary of Hachette Book Group, Inc.
2300 Chestnut Street
Philadelphia, PA 19103-4371

www.runningpress.com

Introduction

YOU PLAYED RUGBY IN YOUR DAY. You wore your black eyes and shoulder dislocations like badges of honor. You can't count how many times you got stepped on in a ruck, or found dirt or grass in weird crevices of your body. Or maybe you're still a player, prioritizing pride over pain, playing the is-it-mud-or-is-it-a-bruise game when you clean yourself off after a match. You take pride in the say-ing "Football is 90 minutes pretending you're hurt, rugby is 80 minutes pretending you're not."

There are times when you need a break from all that, when it's useful to have your body whole and not aching. But you still want the fun, the high of a kick that lands, the support of your teammates. This is where *Desktop Rugby* comes in.

Now you can avoid the tries and the many lacerations that go with them. In *Desktop Rugby*, you skip right to the conversions. With just a flick of your fingers, you can experience the glory of a conversion by aiming our tiny rugby ball through the mini-goal posts. Take turns trying for two-pointers with your office mates . . . this time without the need for a post-match session with deep heat.

Desktop Rugby comes with a goal, ball, tee, and a set of boots. The sight of the post on your office desk is sure to send a challenge to the workers around you. Soon, they'll want to show you that they have what it takes. Maybe you'll get a whole league going. But don't worry—just keep practicing your finger dexterity and you'll stay on top.

A History of Rugby

NO ONE KNOWS EXACTLY HOW rugby started. Some say it can be traced all the way back to an Ancient Greek game called *episkyros*, which later evolved into *harpastum*, a ball game that was played in the Roman Empire. The exact rules of *harpastum* are not known, but we do know it involved a small ball that was similar in size to a modern-day softball. We also know that feet weren't used much, but wrestling moves were frequent. Athenaeus, a rhetorician, wrote of the game, "Great are the exertion and fatigue attendant upon contests of ball-playing, and violent twisting and turning of the neck."

Sounds about right.

There's another origin story for rugby, set much later, in 1823. On a field in the Rugby School, a boarding school in Rugby (which is in Warwickshire, England), some school boys were playing British football. Then, a boy named William Webb Ellis caught a football in his arms and began to run with it. There's no evidence to prove this legend actually happened, but people love it. There's even a statue of William Webb Ellis at The Rugby School, depicting the boy mid-run with a ball in his hand and the winners of the Rugby World Cup are awarded the William Webb Ellis trophy.

Whether or not the story is true,

the Rugby School was important to the growth of the game. Many of the terms we use today, like "offside," originated on the pitch of that school. And in 1845, three Rugby School boys wrote out the first recorded rules of "football" in the Rugby style.

As Rugby students grew up and graduated, they spread their version of football to other towns, and the schoolyard game turned into matches played by men. The first club was started at Cambridge University in 1839, and, helped by the growth of the railroad industry, the game spread across Britain. Throughout the mid-1800s, it spread from there to Australia, Canada, and to American college campuses (where the game evolved into American football).

During this time period, rugby rules weren't clearly established. Usually, they were discussed and agreed upon immediately before a match. There was also confusion around the term "football." Some played a version of football that only involved handling the ball with their feet, while others played football in the "Rugby style" which allowed for carrying and tossing the ball.

This finally came to a head in a meeting in 1863. Eleven clubs came together to establish a clear set of football laws so they could play each other without dispute. The compromise they reached eliminated running with the ball.

The Blackheath Football Club, which favored "running with the ball in the hands toward the opposite goal after a fair catch," withdrew from the football association, and other clubs followed suit. This started the official split between Association Football (soccer) and Rugby Football (rugby).

There was another split coming. The Industrial Revolution spread the game from elite schools to mills and factories, and soon, rugby matches became associated with town and factory pride. Professionalism became an issue. Some believed workers injured during rugby matches should receive compensation for their work lost. Others believed that compensating players could lead to recruiting from the more well-off clubs, detracting from the fairness of the sport. The game split into two types: rugby league and rugby union. Though they were initially only different in administration, both games changed over time, and they now have different laws. Rugby league, popular in Northern England and Australia, involves only thirteen players and uncontested tackles. The tackled player's team must move back ten meters after the tackle. Rugby union is a more popular game worldwide, and in it, the tackle is contested on the ground in rucks.

Today, rugby union is played in over one-hundred countries. The Rugby World Cup, held every four years, is the third most watched world championship, after the Soccer World Cup and Summer Olympics. Women's rugby has also expanded tremendously in the past two decades and is a growing college sport in the U.S.

Desktop Rugby isn't as complex as rugby union, but it does let you be part of the trend, even when you can't make it onto the pitch! Bring rugby's famous spirit of respect and competition to your workplace by getting everyone involved in the action.

Playing Desktop Rugby

"RUGBY IS A GAME FOR HOOLI- gans played by gentlemen," but we call *Desktop Rugby* a sport for all. Seriously, your dog could probably play it. We provide two sets of laws for matches, but feel free to spin a few of your own. There's no RFU to stop you.

LAWS
SINGLE PLAYER

The beauty of *Desktop Rugby* is that it need not be competitive. If you're a rugger fan with sports-hating squares for colleagues, keep your mind on the game by simply using *Desktop Rugby* to practice your conversions.

First, give yourself a time limit. Maybe set the timer on your phone to the ten minutes before your lunch break ends. Set up the goal twenty inches back from the tee, place the ball on the tee, and use your thumb and forefinger to try and flick the ball toward the goal. Every goal scored gets you two points, and every goal missed subtracts two. This way, every time you practice, you're playing against your own highest score.

If you get to the point where you're hitting high scores of 2,000, and your partner informs you that you're flicking imaginary rugby balls in your sleep, congratulations. It's time to make the match a little harder.

Did you notice the miniature boots in the box? They're not just for effect. For a harder level of single-player *Desktop Rugby*, insert the tips of your index and middle fingers into the boots. This will force you to kick the ball with one finger-foot, like a real player. Same point system applies.

MULTI-PLAYER

If your office mates are the type who aren't afraid to knock heads, it's time to get them involved. As a recruiting strategy, we recommend having your rugby set ready to go in a prominent place on your desk. It's a good conversation starter. To coworkers who ask, "Is that a tiny rugby ball?" reply, "*Is* it?" and flick the ball into the goalpost. Then say, "I just scored."

Once you're known around the

office as That Dude with the rugby desk set, it's time to start recruiting. If your coworkers aren't already rugby fans, you'll have to look for less obvious signs that they might be good at the game.

TRAITS TO LOOK FOR IN RECRUITS

★ Talking over people in meetings. This bulldozing attitude could make for a good forward.

★ Walking really fast down hallways. People who do this know how to stay focused in the goal area, even if the goal area in this case is the bathroom.

- ★ The person who responds to your email by presenting a different idea and CC-ing your boss clearly has a strong competitive spirit.

- ★ Looking like you haven't showered in a few days could be a sign that you aren't afraid to get dirty.

- ★ Fast typing abilities could signify finger dexterity, which is helpful for *Desktop Rugby* in particular.

★ And don't forget, multi-player *Desktop Rugby* doesn't have to apply to office settings alone. It could work for any communal area, like a home desk or table.

GAMEPLAY

Forget tries and penalties! This simple miniature match is all about conversions. There isn't real tackling in this game, as it's tough to tackle using only your fingers, but you can get into the spirit of rugby in how you decide which team kicks first. You can decide with a timed thumb war between team captains or a finger scrum. In a scrum, team captains must place their hands against each other in an open half-fist which meets at the knuckles. This should be directly over the ball on the tee. Teammates can place their half fists behind their team captains for additional support. Count to three, then push against each other. The team that pushes the ball entirely behind their line of fists gets to kick first.

In alternating teams, each player gets to kick the ball toward the goal post. Each goal scored grants its team two points. There are no subtracting points in this version of the game. The team with the highest points at the end of everyone's turn is the victor.

As per rugby tradition, end your match by applauding for

the winner. Then drink at a pub, and get rowdy enough to sing. Or, if your office circumstances prevent this level of merriment, hit up the vending machine and email both teams a YouTube clip of a rugby song afterward.

Rugby Trivia

DID YOU KNOW THAT . . .

The first rugby balls were made from pig bladders and leather casings. They were created for the Rugby School by a man named William Gilbert. His nephew James, known for his lung power, had the lucky job of inflating all the bladders.

Before 2016, the rugby Olympic champion was . . . the United States! But only because of the technicality that the U.S. won the gold medal in the 1924 Summer Olympics, and the sport was dropped from the Olympics right after.

The oldest player in the history of the World Cup is Diego Ormaechea from Uruguay. He was captain at forty years old in 1999.

The New Zealand national rugby team, the "All Blacks," perform a traditional ancestral war cry, dance, or challenge of the Māori people—before their international matches.

Speaking of New Zealand, the country's player, Grant Fox, has the record for the most points in one World Cup tournament: 126.

The same whistle has been used for the opening match of the World Cup since 1905. It was originally the whistle of Gil Evans, a Welsh referee.

Rugby rejoins the Summer Olympics in Brazil in 2016! It's the first time the game has hit Olympic heights in 92 years.

This book has been bound
using handcraft methods and
Smyth-sewn to ensure durability.

Written by Eve Legato.

Package designed by Sarah Pierson.

Interior designed by Amanda Richmond.

Edited by Zachary Leibman.

The text was set in
Sport Script and Avenir.